DOTS
on the
FLOOR
and a whole lot more...

Tips and Techniques for Teachers

...... Cathy Spieler ......

Illustrated by
Becky Radtke

CPH
SAINT LOUIS

Copyright © 2000 Concordia Publishing House
3558 S. Jefferson Avenue, St. Louis, MO 63118-3968
Manufactured in the United States of America

1 2 3 4 5 6 7 8 9 10   09 08 07 06 05 04 03 02 01 00

CONTENTS

INTRODUCTION

Using this Book ...

The title of this book comes from an idea I have been using for several years in my own classroom. Lining up is not necessarily one of the life lessons that must be learned in order to succeed. Yet teachers in early childhood classrooms must often get their class to do just that in order to move safely from one location to another. *Dots on the Floor and a Whole Lot More* was born out of a need to get the task done as painlessly and appropriately as possible.

The role of the early childhood educator in a Christian context is extremely important in the life of a child. The life lessons a child needs to learn about living a Christian life are now extended beyond the walls of home and into the classroom. The early childhood educator is a Christian role model for every child taught.

This book is not intended to be used as a curriculum guide. Rather, it can be used as a tool to help utilize time with children to its fullest. Take the opportunity to view instruction and classroom management as a whole rather than parts. The ideas presented here may not be appropriate for all ages within each setting; therefore, consider the age of the children and adapt activities when necessary.

Use this book as a catalyst for new and appropriate ideas. Some ideas may even be ones already used. This book is meant to assist new as well as experienced educators by presenting ideas that have stood the test of time.

It is my hope that this book will help early childhood educators in their pursuit of Christian content and guidance for their classrooms, as well as providing help with organizational skills that will make their task a little easier.

Cathy Spieler

... And a Whole Lot More

Enlarging Patterns

Many of the patterns in this book will be too small. Patterns can be enlarged by increasing the size on a copy machine or taking the pattern to a copying service with large enough machines to meet your needs.

You can also use an overhead transparency to increase the pattern size. Some copiers will print the pattern onto a transparency, or you can trace the pattern directly onto the transparency with a marker. After the transparency is prepared, secure paper of the desired size to a wall. Project the image of the pattern onto the paper, trace the enlarged pattern, and cut it out.

Making Stencils

To make a stencil, enlarge the pattern as earlier directed. Protect your working surface and use an X-Acto knife to cut away the inside shape of the pattern while preserving the outside edges as a frame. If using a scissors, poke a hole in the center and cut toward and around the outside edges. Choose heavy paper, poster board, or plastic to allow the stencil to be used several times.

Position the stencil, tape it in place, and fill the open pattern with color. Remove the stencil when the color is dry.

Recruiting Volunteers

Enlist help with the tasks in this book, starting with the parents of your students. Volunteering encourages them to feel needed as a valuable part of their child's educational experience.

Others to recruit include:

- grandparents
- teenagers (some need service hours for high school, scouts, and other organizations)
- senior adults

Ask for help via your classroom newsletter, church newsletters, or church bulletins. You may be surprised by the response received.

Teacher:

Patterns can be made more sturdy for tracing by laminating them or using heavy stock paper that will stand up to repeated use.

DOTS on the FLOOR

While solid colors work best, patterned paper can also be used for "dots on the floor." Use self-adhesive paper to cut circles that are at least 9″ in diameter.

After cutting, remove the adhesive backing and place the circles on the floor where you would like the children to form a line. Arrange them far enough apart to avoid the pushing and shoving that often occurs when children line up. The circles will adhere to the floor and will only need to be removed if they become worn.

Teach me Your way, O LORD; lead me in a straight path.
Psalm 27:11

Teacher:

This idea can be used for children thru second grade. Children often don't understand what might happen if they line up too close to one another. They may not easily forgive the child that has accidentally stepped on their toes.

NUMBERS on the FLOOR

Follow the directions on the preceding page. Use paint markers that are available in craft or art stores to draw numbers on the circles before securing them to the floor. Permanent felt tip markers will work, but the color is not as vivid, and will wear off more quickly.

Number Activity 1

As the children line up, ask each child to stand on a specific number. The numbers requested do not need to be in numerical order. This activity will aid the children in the identification of numbers as well as prevent the battle of who stands in a particular position.

Number Activity 2

Allow each child to draw a numeral out of a bag or box. They must stand on the numbered dot on the floor that matches the number they have drawn.

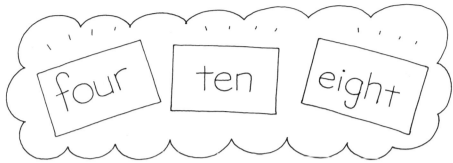

Number Activity 3

Spell out numbers on cards. Allow each child to draw a number card out of a bag or box. They must stand on the corresponding numeral. The child may need help recognizing the spelled number.

Number Activity 4

For children who are ready, use number sentences that equal the numbered spaces on the floor, such as, 4+2, 6+4, or 5-3.

... He set my feet on a rock and gave me a firm place to stand.   Psalm 40:2b

SHAPES on the FLOOR

Enlarge the patterns on the following pages and use the same adhesive paper to make shapes for seasonal cut-outs or theme-related shapes. Apples, pumpkins, turkeys, angels, dinosaurs, gingerbread men, are all examples of shapes that could be used. Use the following shape patterns or design your own to enhance your curriculum.

Outlining Centers

Choose shapes that represent the activity being done in a particular center and create a boundary for that center. For example, paint easels cut out of adhesive paper could be placed on the floor to outline the painting center. Silverware could outline the kitchen play area. Book shapes could outline the reading center, and large raindrops could designate where water activities are done.

Making Boundaries for Play Areas

Use shapes on the floor to indicate spaces of the room where children are allowed to play with large toys such as tricycles, cars, or wagons. Make a pattern showing that type of toy and outline the acceptable play area. Accidentally running into or over this boundary will certainly not cause any damage, but it will help the child notice how far he should go.

Designating Storage Areas

Ask each child to choose something such as a favorite animal or food. Make these shapes and place them on the floor in front of each child's cubby or storage area. This will create instant ownership of the space. If the child is allowed to choose a favorite shape on a home visit or preschool interview, it will help the child feel secure in a new place and help build a trusting relationship between the child and teacher.

Show me Your ways, O Lord, teach me Your paths.
Psalm 25:4

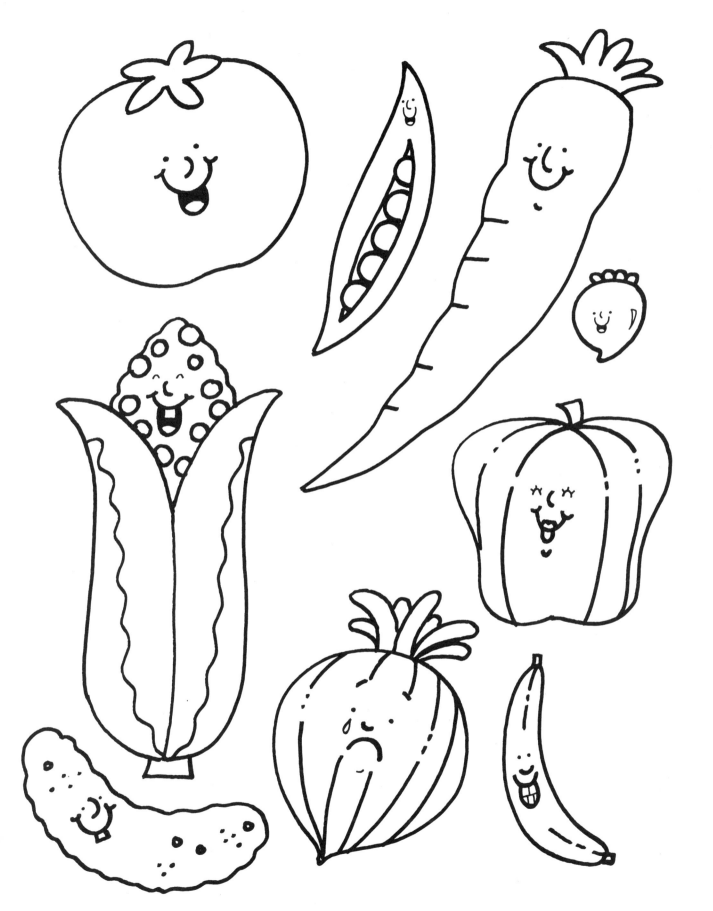

FOOTPRINTS on the FLOOR

Waiting-in-Line Footprints

Make copies of the pattern and cut out child-sized footprints from adhesive paper. Or, trace around the feet of a child to make your own pattern. If right and left are part of your curriculum, add R and L to the footprints.

Place the footprints on the floor in places where children will be standing in line—at the sink, drinking fountain, or in front of the door. Place the footprints a comfortable distance apart to avoid crowding.

Follow the Footprints

Make a trail of footprints in hallways for children to follow as they move from one place to another. Alternate right and left footprints and use different colors leading to different destinations—blue leads to the gym, red leads to the bathroom, etc.

Roundup Footprints

Arrange sets of footprints in a circle to create a space for "Jesus Time" or circle games. Having the children sit or stand on the footprints lends to immediate organization.

Teacher:

If you use foot-shaped note paper, enlarge that shape and use as a pattern. To get footprints that are the size of your children, trace around their own feet. The footprints can even be labeled with their names.

To guide our feet into the path of peace.   Luke 1:79b

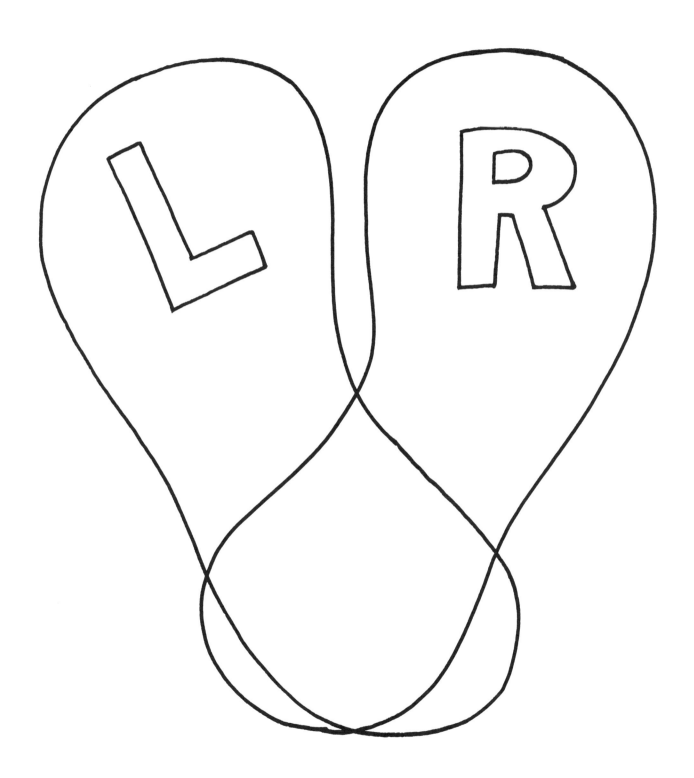

STARS on the FLOOR

Another way to make the children in your class feel special is to have them make their own walk of fame. This activity will also help each child think about the blessings God has provided and how He has made each one special. This would make a great culminating activity for use at the end of a unit.

Enlarge the pattern and cut out one star for each child. Encourage the children to decorate their stars in a personal way. Ideas include drawing pictures of themselves, drawings of activities they enjoy, and personal photographs. Have collage art items available such as glue, pieces of ribbon, buttons, sequins, and glitter.

When finished, have each child tell you about their individual stars. Write their words on the stars. Older children can be encouraged to write their own descriptions on their stars.

Use clear adhesive paper to attach these stars to the floor of your classroom or the hallway leading to the classroom. If you cannot use the floor for this activity, display the stars on a wall or bulletin board.

Teacher:

Adapt this activity by having each child make their own mobile. Duplicate the star pattern in several sizes. Have each child add their picture and name to a large star. Smaller stars could feature talents or gifts from God such as family, friends, athletic abilities or sports interests, special traits, etc.

Shine like stars in the universe as you hold out the Word of Life. Philippians 2:15b–16a

COMPUTER KEYBOARD
on the FLOOR

Teacher:

If your classroom floor is not large enough, assemble the keyboard onto a 4' x 8' sheet of masonite or plywood. Very large versions of the keyboard could be made on two sheets. These sheets could then be hinged together or simply placed next to each other on the playground. Store the large keyboard in an easily accessible area until needed.

This project requires a large open space. A keyboard is generally 3 times as wide, from right to left, as it is from top to bottom (space bar positions). Look for an area that is approximately 3' x 9' or 4' x 12'.

Cut from adhesive paper the appropriate number of pieces to match your computer keyboard. Mark the pieces with the numbers, letters, and any other markings that appear on your computer keyboard.

Place the paper keys directly to the floor in the same arrangement as the computer keyboard. If you use a computer in your classroom, be sure to match that keyboard configuration when you design your own.

Ask the children to stand or jump on designated keys in order to learn the position of the keys, or to reinforce recognition of letters and numbers. Children can move from one letter to another to spell their names. If they are learning to spell other words, use this same activity to reinforce their spelling skills. Have them name each letter as they move from one to the other.

This activity can be adapted by having the children toss bean bags onto the keyboard from the position of the space bar.

Let the wise listen and add to their learning. Proverbs 1:5a

CARPETING on the FLOOR

Carpet on the floor may make the previous ideas seem difficult to use. Following are some ideas for adaptation, or think of your own. Creativity and flexibility are always appropriate!

Carpet Runners

Rather than putting dots on the carpet, use a carpet runner that can be removed and stored. Carpet runners are available in various lengths in discount stores or by the running foot at building supply stores.

Adhesive patterns can be placed directly on the piece of carpet runner. Or, stencils of chosen patterns can be cut and placed onto the runner. Use spray paint or stencil paint and brushes to fill in the stencils.

Roll out the carpet runner as needed for class days and store it when not needed. Be sure to secure the corners of the runner with tape to avoid tripping.

Vinyl Runners

Clear vinyl runners that have been manufactured to protect carpeting can also be used. These work especially well in hallways that lead children to other destinations. Apply adhesive shapes or use stencils to make shapes, letters, or numbers on the vinyl. Permanent marking pens can also be used.

Carpet Samples

Squares of carpet samples are often available from carpet dealers. Check in your church and community for a carpet installer or flooring store that might be able to donate leftover pieces of carpeting or discontinued carpet samples.

Guide me in Your truth and teach me, for You are God my Savior, and my hope is in You all day long.
Psalm 25:5

Teacher:

There are a variety of ways to use carpet squares. They can be used as individual stepping-stones or even as the keys to your computer keyboard. Allow older children to put numbers in numerical order, letters in alphabetical order, or find the letters in their name and assemble a large walk on their name. Let your imagination run wild!

GAMES on the FLOOR

Make up life-size games for the children to play.
Use your imagination!

Giant Puzzle

Make a giant puzzle by taping the backside of several carpet samples together. Use a permanent marker, or paints and stencils, to create a design or geometric shapes on the front of the taped-together piece. Remove the tape and invite the children to reassemble the puzzle.

Animal Game

Help children learn to recognize the difference between pets, farm animals, zoo animals, and those that live in the wild. Draw or attach pictures of different animals on carpet samples. Arrange the carpet samples in any order—circle, line, zig zag, etc.

Make a spinner with the pictures of the different environments where animals might live—home, farm, zoo, jungle, trees, etc. Have each child spin and stand on the picture of an animal that might live in that particular environment.

Variations:

- *Make a large spinner to use on the floor.*
- *Put the environments on the carpet squares and the animals on the spinner.*
- *Write words like FARM, ZOO, and PET on the spinner instead of using pictures.*
- *Number the carpet samples and ask the children to keep track of the numbers on which they land.*

CLIP IT

Do you lose the notes sent to you in the clutter of your desk? Do you have trouble finding the key to the storage closet? Or maybe you need a special place to send notes to parents as they pick up their children. Use that age-old invention—the clothespin.

Wooden clothespins with a spring have many uses:

- *Glue one of these to the side of your filing cabinet and use it for clipping together the notes you get each morning.*

- *Attach a clothespin to the storage closet and hang the keys on it until you return the items you were using.*

- *Place a clothespin above the coat hook of each child. Special notes or important parent information will be easily seen when the child is picked up from school.*

- *Glue a small magnet to the back of a spring-type clothespin. Send these home to be put on refrigerators so that important school information can have a special place at home.*

- *Place a clothespin outside your classroom door for attendance information that is picked up by the office.*

Teacher:

If you do not wish to use glue, try Velcro dots. They are available with adhesive already on the back. Note that the clothespins can be labeled with the names of children or with words indicating how they are to be used.

... [I] delight to see how orderly you are and how firm your faith in Christ is.

Colossians 2:5

CONTAIN IT

What teacher of young children does not have a storage problem? We are well-known as collectors. The following ideas will help organize the materials you use for teaching and those the children use.

Containing Teacher's Things

Ideas for organizing and storing your teaching materials include:

- *Cardboard boxes, painted and labeled*
- *Plastic hooks on the wall*
- *Plastic laundry baskets*
- *Wicker baskets*
- *Plastic containers from cat food or laundry detergent*

Teacher:

Use your imagination and find creative ways to store the containers. For example, stack cardboard boxes to create boundaries between centers and areas in your classroom.

But everything should be done in a fitting and orderly way.
1 Corinthians 14:40

Containing Children's Things

If children have small personal materials such as crayons or markers, they will need to have a place to put them. Some ways to store these include:

- *Purchased school-box*
- *Covered orange juice can*
- *Painted and decorated tin can with sharp edges removed*
- *Plastic drinking cup, decorated and labeled*
- *Plastic shoebox*
- *Cottage cheese or yogurt container*

If children are required to keep track of larger personal items, ideas for storage include:

- *Plastic crates*
- *Cardboard boxes, decorated and labeled*
- *Large ice-cream tubs from an ice-cream store*
- *Large tin cans hung on the wall with a rope handle*

File Your Own Work

There is often a need to save work done by each child. Parent-Teacher conferences, school open houses, or portfolio assessments create a need to keep individual files for each child. Once children learn to recognize their own name, they can be encouraged to file their own pictures and pages of work.

Create a filing system that best suits the abilities of the children in your classroom. A narrow box or crate will work well. Place each child's decorated file folder in the crate. Placing small pictures on the tab portion of the file folder, along with the names, will help young children find their folders more easily. Older children can print their own names on their folders.

Teacher:

Younger children will need more assistance and help in understanding this process. It is worth the effort, however, when the children feel a sense of accomplishment and independence after mastering the process.

My son, if you accept My words and store up My commands within you, turning your ear to wisdom and applying your heart to understanding ...
then you will understand the fear of the LORD and find the knowledge of God. Proverbs 2:1–2, 5

MEMORY BOOK

Save any and all pictures taken throughout the school year. These can be organized by volunteers into an end-of-the-year memory book. Plan ahead to include pictures of the first days of school or some type of beginning-of-the-year group picture.

Take pictures of activities and events including field trips and day-to-day activities. Date and label the pictures as soon as they are developed so that you remember what was happening when a particular picture was taken. Some schools might also use these pictures for yearbooks or to be displayed on a special bulletin board.

As the school year progresses, file pictures for individual children into separate files. At the end of the year, make a memory book for each child by placing their pictures on poster board or heavy paper, featuring one picture per page. Write a caption for each picture that tells what was happening and includes the names of other children pictured. This will help so the memories won't be forgotten.

Place the pictures in chronological order and design a cover with a title naming the school and the class. Three-hole punch the left side of each page and secure the pages together using metal rings or pieces of ribbon.

Teacher:

Some parents may not be able to be actively involved in their child's school experience. These parents, in particular, will appreciate pictures of the rocket ship built with blocks, or the cooking project they could only hear about, or the field trip to the pumpkin farm.

I thank my God every time I remember you. Philippians 1:3

A SCRAPBOOK for YOURSELF

Years go by quickly. As the years go by, they tend to blend together, and the details are not as distinct. As you close each school year, take some time to record the events of the year.

Select several photos of the class, as well as photos of special events and projects from the year. Make several scrapbook pages and include some of your thoughts about the past year.

Teacher:

As you add pages to your scrapbook, you will be recording your own personal teaching history that will bring back many memories in years to come.

I have not stopped giving thanks for you, remembering you in my prayers.

Ephesians 1:16

Cut Your Own Border

Most classrooms have bulletin boards. Teachers are often drawn to the colorful array of preprinted borders available in teacher supply stores. Most of these colorful borders do not, however, communicate that yours is a Christian community.

The following patterns will allow you to clearly display a Christian message to everyone entering your classroom. Make a cardboard template of the pattern you wish to copy. Trace the pattern on construction paper and cut it out. Add additional colors and features, or keep the pattern as a silhouette of the shape.

If preferred, make photocopies of the pattern onto paper. Have the children color, decorate, and cut out the patterns. Staple them around the outside edge of your bulletin boards. Have the children help you determine how many patterns are needed to go around the entire border.

As the mountains surround Jerusalem, so the LORD surrounds His people both now and forevermore.
Psalm 125:2

Teacher:

You may find other uses for these border patterns. They could be used for cutting practice or tracing practice. They could be used for the covers of books or name plates for tables.

STORE-A-BOOK

Teacher:

It is also a good idea to store these library books in a separate place, away from classroom books. Be sure to give children clear directions regarding the handling of books that belong to others.

Keeping Track of Library Books

Teachers often hesitate to allow children to look at library books that have been brought in from the school or public library. The age-old problem of keeping them separated from other books in the classroom always occurs.

One way to avoid this problem is to place each library book in a large, resealable plastic storage bag. After looking at library books, the children are instructed to place them back in the bag. The bags can be stored on a bookshelf or in a crate. This procedure keeps library books separate from classroom books. If a bag is found empty, everyone can help find the missing book.

Library Bags

You can help children keep track of the library books they take home. Buy fabric bags at your local discount store, or plan to have them homemade. Collect fabric remnants or scraps. Recruit a volunteer to sew the fabric into rectangular bags with handles. A good size for the finished bag would be approximately 12" x 16". Write the name of the school and the grade on each bag.

Add a note to each bag reminding both children and parents how to care for library books.

Book Bag

Teacher:

Library books can easily get mixed in with books children may already have at home. Using the library bags will help families keep track of those school library books. Remind them to keep the library books in the bag when not reading them.

Jesus did many other things as well. If every one of them were written down, I suppose that even the whole world would not have room for the books that would be written. John 21:25

33

BACK TO SCHOOL

Little Red Schoolhouse

Copy the pattern to make a little red schoolhouse for each child. Place each child's photograph in the doorway of a schoolhouse. These can be school pictures, photos that were taken on home visits, or pictures brought in by the children.

Add the group of schoolhouses to a bulletin board, welcoming the children. Or reinforce each schoolhouse with a piece of cardboard or poster board, then glue an upside-down spring clothespin on the back. This will allow the schoolhouse to stand on its own so that it can be displayed on a table or shelf.

My School

The above activity can be modified by using the pattern for a modern version of a school. Place the pictures of each child in the individual doorways. If the pattern is enlarged to make one big school, pictures of the children can be displayed in the windows. Plan ahead to make sure there are enough windows for everyone in your class.

You can also draw an outline of your own school by tracing a photograph. Or duplicate actual photographs of your school. Glue a picture of each child onto the individual photographs. Better yet, photograph each child in front of a recognizable area of the school. Send these home as mementos for the children to keep.

Teacher:

Parents enjoy seeing their child's classroom. The schoolhouse picture not only helps parents identify their child's classroom, but becomes a cherished memento of a specific school year.

[Jesus said,] "Let the little children come to Me, and do not hinder them, for the Kingdom of God belongs to such as these."

Mark 10:14b

Name

Name

FIND YOUR NAME

Younger children might need to have their names printed under their photographs until they begin to recognize their own name.

Some children are hesitant, especially at the beginning of the school year, to enter the classroom and get involved. The following activity will draw the children into the classroom and help them feel included in the larger group.

Cut out Christian shapes, seasonal shapes, or ones that correspond with the time of year or current theme in your classroom. Print each child's name on a shape and place the shapes on a table or bulletin board close to the entrance to your classroom.

Encourage each child to find his or her name upon entering the classroom each day, then place it on a table or bulletin board elsewhere in the room. For example, use apples in September and have the children add their apples to a tree across the room. Or write the names on animals and have the children place their animals on the ark with Noah.

Make note of the children who are absent each day. Pray for these children by name. As the children learn to read each others' names, they will also be able to see who is absent or remind a forgetful child to add the apple to the tree.

But rejoice that your names are written in heaven.
Luke 10:20b

SNACK TIME PLACE CARDS

Children are encouraged to learn to recognize the names of the others in their class when they have opportunities to be in charge of the seating arrangement at snack time.

Make a tent-type name card for each child. To decorate the name cards, use the patterns to make food labels, add food stickers, or draw your own. Choose one or two pairs of children each day to arrange the name cards on the tables before snack. As you allow them to decide who they would like to sit next to on that day, they will quickly learn to know and recognize the names of all of the children in their class.

As the children become more and more familiar with each other, they will have an opportunity to demonstrate empathy as they place pairs or groups of friends together.

Teacher:

This task serves several purposes. First, it helps children learn to recognize the names of others. Even if it takes awhile to recognize the names, it gives the children an opportunity to take on responsibility.

Give thanks to the LORD, for He is good; His love endures forever. Psalm 107:1

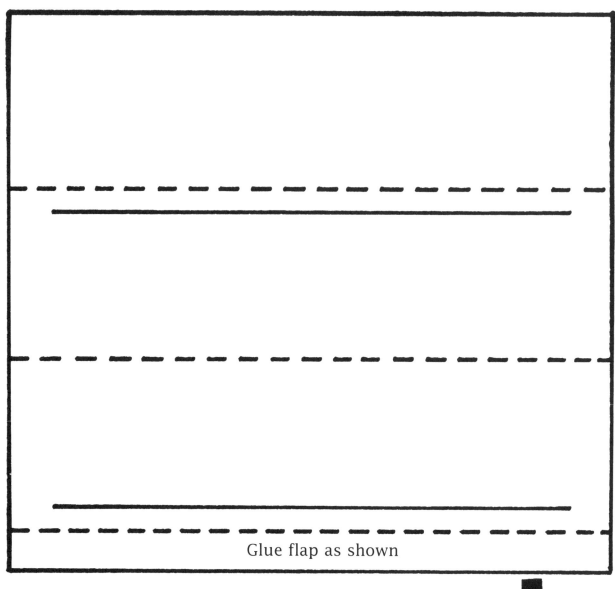

Glue flap as shown

CHILD on the WEEK

Table Display

All children love to have a time set aside when they are the center of attention. One child, per week, could be featured as the Child of the Week. Children could be featured at the time of their birthday, in alphabetical order, or in any order you choose.

Ask each parent to send photographs of their child showing important events and people in their life from birth to the present. Arrange the photographs on a piece of poster board that serves as a frame. Display the pictures and other significant items on a table for all to see.

Teacher:

Be sure to send adequate directions to the parents explaining your request. Give parents plenty of ideas and explain your expectations. It might be wise to post a schedule so that parents have an idea of when their child will be featured as child of the week. Take good care of photographs and personal mementos in order to return them in good condition. Use all pictures and items for display only. Set firm limits with your class so that nothing gets torn or broken.

Bulletin Board Display

During the appropriate week, give each child the opportunity to decorate a small bulletin board with significant pictures and items that tell about themselves. This type of bulletin board is available in several sizes from discount stores.

Send the bulletin board and a note of explanation for the parents home with each child. After adding the items, the bulletin board is brought back for display. (It is best to send the bulletin board home at the end of the prior week in order to allow plenty of time over the weekend for assembly.)

The bulletin board can be covered with colorful fabric or bright paper. Pictures, as well as personal mementos, can be attached to the board. Display the bulletin board in a prominent place. Allow time for children to explain their mementos to the class.

But you are a chosen people, a royal priesthood,
a holy nation, a people belonging to God, that you
may declare the praises of Him who called you
out of darkness into His wonderful light.

1 Peter 2:9

Make Your Own Poster

You may have seen the packages of posters that are commercially available for children to complete as they add information about themselves. This activity will allow the children to create their own poster.

One way to complete the activity is to enlarge the pattern as provided. Have the children fill in the spaces, providing the appropriate information. Encourage them to color and decorate the poster in a creative way.

Consider using Christian shapes such as the dove, shell, fish, church, or cross. Include information such as baptismal birthday and the name of the church or school attended. (Note: Parent involvement is necessary, especially where dates are needed.) This poster could be saved and used as part of the Child of the Week displays.

A second option is to have the children create a collage poster about themselves. Enlarge and copy each section of the pattern, or create your own. Have the children complete each section, cut and arrange them on a piece of poster board or a large piece of paper.

If using this option, the posters can be adapted to connect with a unit theme or include particular types of information. For example, posters made as part of a social studies unit about neighborhoods could include information such as house number, street name, city, and state. Shapes of countries, continents, and the world could also be included.

And so we know and rely on the love God has for us. God is love. Whoever lives in love lives in God, and God in him.   1 John 4:16

All About Me

My birthday:

My name is

My pets:

My favorite toy is

I was baptized (or blessed)

My church

My favorite color

My family

PLAYING with BOXES

Remember watching children play with the boxes from their gifts rather than the gifts themselves? Children seem to love boxes. They are inexpensive and come in many sizes. They also leave room for the imagination to roam.

Large boxes can become play houses by simply cutting out windows and a door. Boxes can be forts, Noah's ark, or ships sailing on the sea. They can be the fire department, the grocery store, or the post office.

When using thematic units, try to incorporate the use of a large box, adding it to the dramatic play area. Transform the box using paint or wallpaper, or covering it with bulletin board or craft paper. Let the children decide what the box will become and what it should look like. The children can paint the large areas and you add the details.

Walls of Jericho

Paint small boxes and decorate as stones. Stack the boxes to make the walls of Jericho. The re-enactment of the story becomes memorable when the wall is toppled at the appropriate time.

Teacher:

Let the children play with the box before changing anything. This will encourage their imaginations and help them decide what to make. Make sure cut edges are not sharp and that all staples are removed.

So then, just as you received Christ Jesus as Lord, continue to live in Him, rooted and built up in Him, strengthened in the faith as you were taught, and overflowing with thankfulness.

Colossians 2:6–7

Designing a Car

Cut out the bottom of a box, or fold the flaps to the inside. On the top, fold one end-flap and tape it to the box to form the front end of the car. Attach an additional piece of cardboard for the windshield. Add painted doors, wheels, and bumpers.

Ask the children to bring in any old knobs, buttons, or gizmos from home. Paint the outside of the car with silver paint, or cover it with aluminum foil or metallic wrapping paper. Attach all kinds of knobs, buttons, switches, levers, or gauges to the inside walls, resembling instruments. (Attach the items with a hot glue gun or wire through the side of the box. Be sure to remove all sharp edges.)

The Ark

Make an ark in a corner of your classroom. Tape long pieces of cardboard together for the sides. Lean a real board against it for a ramp. Add small boxes for animal pens, and place several animals in the pens and along the walls of the ark. Allow the children to bring stuffed animals to place in the ark.

PUPPET THEATERS

Puppet theaters can also be made from boxes. The theaters can be designed in many shapes and sizes depending upon the box you have and the size of the puppets that will be used.

Cut an opening on one side of the box to create the stage. Be sure this opening is cut near the top of the box. Attach a small piece of the cut-out section to make a shelf at the bottom of the opening. Glue, staple, or attach a piece of fabric over the opening for a stage curtain. Remove the entire back side of the box so the children can get in and out of the puppet stage easily. Paint and decorate the box as desired. This is a great project for the children.

Small puppet theaters can be set up on a table. Large ones will sit on the floor with the puppet masters sitting inside the box. Small puppet theaters are great for finger puppets and puppets made from wooden spoons. Large puppet theaters are better for the more traditional hand puppets. Have the children act out their Bible stories for each other.

Teacher:

Puppet theaters can be added to enhance a unit or can be in the dramatic play area of your classroom. Allow children freedom to make up their own puppet plays in addition to retelling Bible stories or theme-related stories.

Be imitators of God, therefore, as dearly loved children and live a life of love, just as Christ loved us and gave Himself up for us as a fragrant offering and sacrifice to God.

Ephesians 5:1–2

PUPPETS

Young children can make their own puppets for retelling Bible stories. These puppets can be made and used at school, then sent home. The children can be encouraged to use them to share the Bible story with their family.

Puppet-Making Center

To establish a puppet-making center, designate an area and have a variety of materials available. Gather materials such as leftover fabric trim, wiggle eyes, fake fur, yarn, and odd buttons. Wooden spoons, small plastic disposable spoons, cardboard circles, and gloves can all be used to make great puppets.

To help organize the puppet-making process, use a 3″ x 5″ index card, or larger, to diagram the directions for the children. Place the card in the center and allow the children to create their own puppets.

Use your creativity to come up with puppet ideas. Animal figures drawn and cut out could be used for Noah and the ark. Spoons in different sizes could be used for David and Goliath. Cardboard or heavy paper circles, decorated with crayon and construction paper, may be a good way to start.

Finger Puppets

Copy the patterns provided or design your own. Have the children color and cut out the puppet. A simple bubble shape can be drawn around the puppet to help young children who might have difficulty cutting around the intricate design. After cutting, fold the bands back and tape them together, making a ring to slip over a young child's finger.

The same patterns can also be used to make larger puppets to fit over a hand. Enlarge the pattern and follow the same directions as outlined above.

Teacher:

Younger children will most likely need more help with this activity. Older children may be able to make the puppets more easily by themselves if you do one set together, then let them create the next set on their own.

I praise You because I am fearfully and wonderfully made; Your works are wonderful, I know that full well.
Psalm 139:14

48

PROGRAM IDEAS

Act Out a Book

If the end-of-the-year program is coming too quickly and you don't know what to do, choose a favorite book of the class and turn the book into a play.

Most picture books lend themselves easily to this process. An example of a book that works well is *The Very Quiet Cricket* by Eric Carle. Use poster board to make shapes resembling the artwork done by the illustrator. (Remember not to copy the illustrations exactly as that would constitute copyright infringement.) Hold up each picture as the children act out the story.

Feature the children as the characters in the book by cutting an open space in the poster board for their faces. The children can look out through the hole as they carry the poster board and appear on stage at the appropriate time. Your job is to read the story, and the children will make it come alive.

Vary this activity by making headbands for each child. Have them dress in clothing of a color that resembles the animal or object they are portraying.

Sing It Out

There are many songs that can be acted out as well. Songs with animals and characters are easily acted out and presented at programs. For example, children love singing songs such as *If I Were a Butterfly*. Making poster board animals and lining them up in order, will help the children remember which animal comes next in the song. To assist in learning the song, you may want to make a smaller version of the animal pictures to use as flash cards.

Teacher:

Make sure you practice with the poster board figures. They are hard to manage for small hands. The posters can be made in various sizes. Choose a size that works best for each child.

I will praise You, O LORD, among the nations; I will sing of You among the peoples. Psalm 57:9

WALL-SIZED MURALS

When doing a play or planning for a unit with a particular theme, we often look for ways to convert the classroom or stage into a setting that will reinforce the topic. What a great time to let the children help!

You and the children can create wall-sized murals even if you are not very artistic. Copy one of the patterns onto an overhead transparency. Cover one of the walls with paper. Place the transparency on an overhead projector and project the pattern onto the paper. Trace the lines with pencil or marker. The image may be made as large or small as you wish.

The patterns provided are just suggestions. You can also trace other pictures or scenes directly onto the transparency. This creates a wide variety of possibilities.

Teacher:

After the pattern has been traced, allow the children to help paint or color the scene. Place it on the floor or on a low table. You might consider sponge-painting parts of the mural to create interesting textures. Sections of the mural could be traced separately and finished before adding them to the background.

[The LORD] has made everything beautiful in its time.
He has also set eternity in the hearts of men; yet they cannot fathom what God has done from beginning to end.
Ecclesiastes 3:11

FOLDED GREETING CARDS

There are several occasions when making a special greeting card is most appropriate. An attractive greeting card with a surprise inside will be fun for the children to make.

Folded greeting cards can be made by photocopying one of the patterns provided or creating your own design. Have the children color and decorate the design. Then cut on the solid lines and fold on the dotted lines. (Some children will probably need help with both the cutting and the folding.)

As a final step, choose a small straight area on the outside of the pattern to fold the entire card in half. This will allow the cut-out design to pop out when the card is opened.

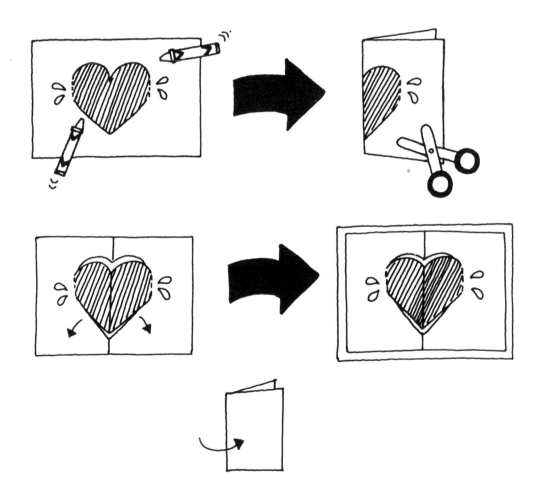

Not one of them is forgotten by God. Luke 12:6b

Make Your Own Stamps

Rubber stamps and ink stamp pads have many uses. They can be stamped on pages to indicate a job well done, and they can also be used to create artistic patterns, math problems, and one-of-a-kind note cards.

There are many rubber stamps commercially available; however, many are rather costly. You can make your own stamps very simply, with just a few materials. The design may not be as intricate; however, you will have the advantage of making stamps to fit your individual needs. You could even make a set of stamps with basic shapes and let the children use these shapes to create their own special pictures. Any stamps created could also be used to make greeting cards or invitations to that special parent program.

First, you will need some small wooden blocks. Scraps from a previous woodworking project will work; but make sure the edges of the wood are sanded smooth. You will also need adhesive-backed latex foam padding that is sold for use in shoes.

Trace one of the patterns provided, or any design you wish, onto the paper side of the padding. (Remember that this will be a mirror-image of the stamp itself.) Cut out the shape you have traced. Remove the paper backing and stick the cut-out shape onto the wooden block.

Teacher:

The latex padding may be difficult for children to cut. Because of this, it might be better for you to create the stamps and let the children use them. You might ask for their ideas about the shapes or figures they would like you to make.

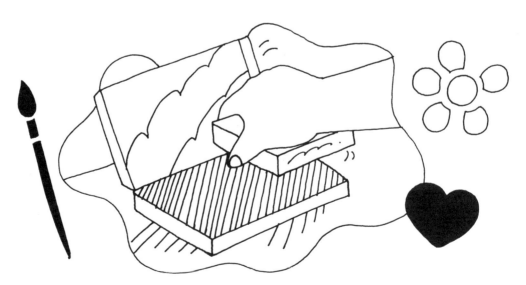

All who are skilled among you are to come and make everything the Lord has commanded.

Exodus 35:10

FAMILY TREE

Make a take-home family tree as part of a unit on family, or as a unique gift for Mother's Day. The method described here makes use of homemade rubber stamps. To make these stamps, follow the directions provided on previous pages.

To make the tree, make a rubber stamp using the trunk pattern provided below. Paint the tree trunk on the rubber stamp with brown tempera paint. Press the tree stamp in the lower center of a piece of paper. Use a green crayon or tempera paint to draw an outline of the treetop.

The children can make leaves by pressing their index finger into green tempera paint and pressing fingerprints inside the outline of the treetop. A green ink pad will also work well.

To make the apples, make a rubber stamp using the apple pattern provided. Paint the apple on the rubber stamp with red tempera paint. Stamp one apple for each member of the family. When dry, write the name of each person in the family on an apple.

When the entire project is finished, print the last name of the family beside the tree. Print **MY FAMILY TREE** on the other side of the tree.

Teacher:

This project can be done in several stages so that the paint can dry between each step. These make nice gifts if framed with a cardboard mat.

He and all his family were devout and God-fearing; he gave generously to those in need and prayed to God regularly.   Acts 10:2

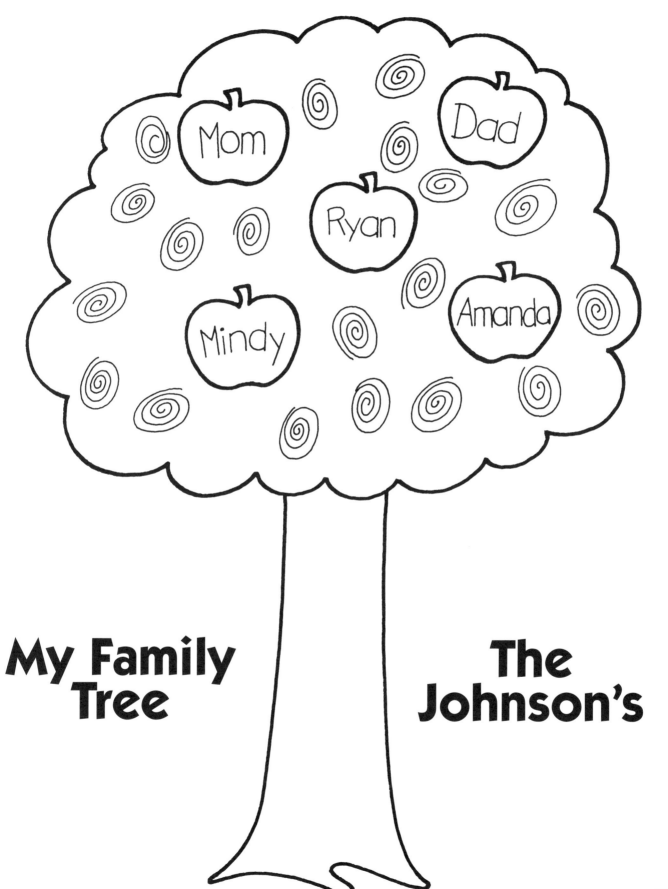

My Family Tree

The Johnson's

FRAME IT

Children love to make small gifts to take home. It is sometimes difficult to come up with items that are inexpensive and easy for children to make. Most parents love to get pictures. School pictures and photographs taken during school activities or on field trips can become treasured mementos.

Paper Doily Frames

Small paper doilies can be used with this project. Cut pieces of brightly colored poster board into two circles slightly larger than the doily. Glue the doily to one circle so the bright color shows through the doily design. Cut out a window for the child's picture. Cut the window to a size slightly smaller than the picture itself. Tape the picture behind the window so that the child's face shows through the opening. Glue the other poster board circle onto the back. Add a strip of poster board to the back of the frame to make a stand.

Lucite Frames

A more expensive way to frame pictures is with decorated acrylic frames. These small thin frames are available at discount craft stores. Purchase or collect a variety of buttons, beads, sequins, ribbons, lace, sequins, or other small objects that can be glued onto the frame. Small stickers will also work. Allow the children to decorate the outer edges, or the top and bottom of the frame. Slip a picture in the slot between the front and back.

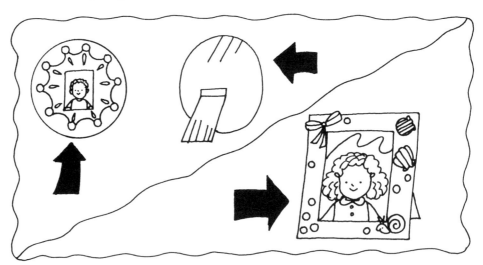

I became a servant of this gospel by the gift of God's grace given me through the working of His power.

Ephesians 3:7

NOTES and NOTICES

Communication with parents, recognition of children's accomplishments, and notification of problems are all a crucial part of effective teaching.

Give your letters you send home with the children a professional look. Use a special heading and/or border to distinguish your notes from others sent home. Copy and use the following pages as needed. The suggestions given may even spark ideas to help you create your own notes and notices that will meet your individual classroom needs. Copy these in advance and keep a supply ready to use. You might want to color code them by copying the individual pages on different colors of paper.

Children may also enjoy receiving special recognition in the form of a note from the teacher. These can be displayed in a place of honor at home or kept as a remembrance.

Teacher:

Even though the parent may bring the child to the classroom or pick them up at the end of class, it is not always easy to communicate the accomplishments or problems of the day. Personal contact is always the best, but sometimes it is more efficient to communicate in written form.

You yourselves are our letter, written on our hearts, known and read by everybody.   2 Corinthians 3:2

Notes and Notices

Field Trip Permission Slip

To the parents of _____ ,

Our class will be going on a field trip to _____

_____ .

The field trip will take place on _____

_____ .

We will leave school at _____ and return at _____ .

We will use _____ as the means of transportation.

☐ We will need volunteer drivers.

Your child will need to bring _____ .

Signed: _____

·····🍎·······🍎·······🍎·······🍎·······🍎·······🍎·······🍎·······🍎·······🍎·····

_____ has permission to attend the above-mentioned field trip.

We will abide by the rules and regulations for field trips as established

by the school.

☐ Yes, I can drive. I can take _____ children in my car.

☐ No, I cannot drive.

_____   _____
Parent or guardian signature   Date

Great Day Notice

_____ had a great day today!

This is what happened: _____

_____

_____ .

You can be so proud!

Signed _____ Date _____

Noteworthy Behavior

_____

☐   Showed kindness to someone

☐   Was very polite

☐   Showed concern for someone

☐   Helped someone

☐   Followed directions well

☐   Demonstrated excellent behavior

Signed _____ Date _____

This Was a Difficult Day

_____ experienced some of the following difficulties today:

- ☐ Appeared sad
- ☐ Did not behave in usual manner
- ☐ Appeared grumpy
- ☐ Had difficulty with a friend
- ☐ Did not follow directions
- ☐ Other: _____

_____ .

Signed _____ Date _____

Please Help

To the parents of _____ ,

In your child's class, we are currently working on _____

_____ .

Your child is experiencing some difficulty with _____

_____ .

Please help by _____

_____ .

Thank You. If you have questions, please let me know.

Signed _____ Date _____

Ideas of My Own